A Walk with the Father

A Walk with the Father

Intimate Relationship

Brenda Williams

Kingdom Living Publishing
Accokeek, MD 20607

Author's photographs by Magic Glamour
www.magicglamour.com

Cover design by Visualarts

Published by

Kingdom Living Publishing
P.O. Box 660
Accokeek, MD 20607

ISBN 978-0-9968089-0-3

Printed in the United States of America.
For worldwide distribution.

Dedication

I dedicate this book to everyone who desires to have an intimate relationship with the Father, Son, and Holy Spirit. To all those who have spoken words of encouragement and prayed for me, this is a result of your labor.

Acknowledgment

To the Holy Spirit, who has drawn me closer to Father God and has helped me to have an intimate relationship with the Father.

To my husband, Willie, who has always supported me and encouraged me in everything I do.

To my children, Tracie and Willie, Jr., who God used to bring me to a place of recognizing that I needed Him to help me be the mother and wife I needed to be.

To my parents, sisters, and brothers, thank you for your constant love and support.

To my late sisters, Mary Janet Black and Effie Whitner, for always having a listening ear, encouraging me to write this book and to be all God created me to be.

To my prayer partners and friends, Helen Trice, Lillie Jackson, Janice Stancil, and Cathy Mincey, who have always prayed for me and with me.

To Women in Fellowship, Inc. for your words of encouragement and prayers; and special thanks to

Stephanie Brown, who edited this book and encouraged me not to quit but to complete the task.

To Hope Christian Church, Bishop Harry R. Jackson, Jr., Senior Pastor, and Dr. Vivian M. Jackson, who teach the Word of God and encourage us to walk it out daily.

Contents

Introduction

While walking one day, I asked the Holy Spirit what the name of my first book should be. He answered, "*A Walk with the Father*."

The Holy Spirit helped me to title and compose this book, *A Walk with the Father*. I believe it will help you to cultivate a relationship with God the Father. The Father is God, and God is love. Love is the very nature of God. He protects and provides for us. He cares about every detail of our lives. He has a purpose and a plan for our lives. He creates and calls each person to a unique purpose and destiny. Yes, the Father loves us.

The Father wants to manifest Himself to every person. The Holy Spirit is gently drawing you closer to the Father, who desires to lead us into a closer relationship with Him. The Holy Spirit is the third person of the Triune Godhead (Matthew 28:19, 2 Corinthians 13:14). The Holy Spirit is God; equal with the Father and Son. The Holy Spirit remains in the earth today to teach and comfort.

Jesus, the Son of God, demonstrated living a life pleasing the Father. He shared and spoke what the Father wanted all to know. The Father also wants every person to come to a saving knowledge of His Son Jesus Christ. Yes, the Father loves us.

Sometimes we do not recognize how important a relationship with the Father is. He wants to have an intimate relationship with us. The more we spend time in worship and the Word, the more we fall in love with Him. We invite Him to speak to our heart. We allow Him to speak to us about our circumstances, and we began to trust Him. We allow His love and compassion to change our hearts, and we want to spend more time with Him. He becomes an integral part of our daily living, just like our friends and family. The more time we spend together, the better we get to know each other. The closer our relationship becomes.

The Father always allows each person the choice to live according to their personal understanding of the Father's way. He wants all of us to trust Him and to be obedient to His Word. We are called to walk in His ways and to love our neighbor as ourselves. If we desire it and cooperate, His love will flow from us to others who will see us as examples and messengers for Him everywhere we go. Every day can be, should be, open to His leading and direction.

Introduction

God loves us so much that He gave His only begotten son for our sins. Why not allow Him to lead and guide us? Our lives would be so much better if we allowed the Father to walk with us every day and if we acknowledged Him in every situation.

In this book, I will share just a small part of what the Father has shown me in my journey with Him. As I look back over my life, I know that He has been with me since the very beginning of my life. He had protected me when I did not even know He existed. He is such a wonderful loving Father. A good father loves, corrects, guides, and disciplines each of his children.

I am so glad He loves me. I have great expectation every day as I walk with Him. I expect Him to speak to me every day, and I expect Him to direct my footsteps. My relationship with Him will never end.

I want you to experience His love in a greater way, to know Him as a loving Father. God, the Father, loves you. I hope you enjoy reading *A Walk with the Father* and that you will allow your walk with Him to enlarge, enrich, and brighten the great journey that He has for you.

Notes and Reflections

My Hunger for More

In 1970, I was a member of a Baptist Church in Washington, D.C., where I was very active. I was a fully engaged member of the Senior Usher Board, Treasurer of the Building Fund Committee, Treasurer of the Mass Choir, and one of the Directors of the Junior Usher Board. I attended just about all the services that the church had. Even though I served in all of those auxiliaries and rarely missed a service, I felt empty. There was something missing. I wanted more. One day I said, "God, there has to be more than this. I go to church; I come back home, and I still feel empty."

Not long after that, I attended a night choir rehearsal. Two people in the choir were arguing, and they were really going at each other. One of the ladies was someone who was always shouting and praising God when we sang outside the church. I went home after seeing them go at each other, screaming at each other in front of everyone, up in each other face. It was very disappointing to see them acting that way; I couldn't believe what I had seen and heard from two people who were supposed to be Christians. I continued to think about how they behaved, and I cried out to God. "I don't want to be like that. I want people to see You in me. I want more; I want more. I want to know You. I want to be in Your presence and know that I am in Your presence."

Over the next several weeks, I started reading the Word more. I attended Sunday School, Baptist Training Union classes, and Bible Study on Saturdays with one of the Sunday school teachers, at her house. While I wanted more, I did not know how to get it. I began to discuss with others my desire for change. One day I talked with Jerry, a deacon at my church. He suggested that I call his wife, my friend Dianne. The next day I called and explained to her how I felt. She told me that I needed the power of God in my life, the baptism of the Holy Spirit with the evidence of speaking in tongues. She added that God would fill the emptiness that I was feeling, and she probably said much more. The power of God in me is what I remembered more than anything, and that was what I wanted.

The following day, she called and wanted to share some Scriptures with me. So I asked my supervisor if I could have an extended lunch. I wanted to go downtown to meet my friend. He encouraged me to take all the time that I needed.

At the lunch meeting, she gave me some Scriptures to meditate on and read. She explained all of the Scriptures to me. Each was about the baptism of the Holy Spirit and the power that each believer can receive. I knew that I could receive this power, and I wanted this power in my life. It was what I was missing; I just knew it. I called another friend, Helen Trice, and shared the Scriptures with her. We both began to read them, and we asked God to fill us with the baptism of the Holy Spirit with the evidence of speaking in tongues.

Continuing to pray the Scriptures about receiving the Holy Spirit a few weeks later, we decided to go to an evening service at Jericho Baptist Church in Washington, D.C. Bishop James R. Peebles and Pastor Betty P. Peebles were the pastors. That night Pastor Betty was teaching from the book of Revelations. At the end of her message, Bishop Peebles gave an altar call, inviting anyone who wanted to receive the baptism of the Holy Spirit, to come down to the front of the church. The teaching and word given applied to us. Helen and I went down to the altar. Bishop Peebles prayed for me, and I was slain in the spirit for the first time; He anointed my head with oil. As he prayed, I felt this power go all over me from the top of my head to my feet. The power of the Holy Spirit was so overwhelming over me that I could not stand up any longer. I began to lift my hands up in the air and praise God verbally in a loud voice. I was crying so hard; I could not stop crying and praising God.

At the church where I was a member, I never saw or spoke with a person who had ever had such an experience. I remember laying there on the floor, thinking to myself, "I know this is not me crying and praising God out loud like this." I could not stop. It seemed like I was on that floor at least twenty minutes. I finally got up and went back to my seat as the service ended. When I got myself together, I asked my friend if she had spoken in tongues and she said no. I told her that I hadn't either. However, I felt so good, so clean, happy, and free. I felt like I did not have a care in the world.

The next day I talked to my friend Dianne and she said that the Holy Spirit was drawing me to Him and that if I asked Him to fill me with the evidence of speaking in tongues, He would. On Sunday, January 15, l984, I attended a service with Dianne at Free Gospel Deliverance Temple, where Bishop Ralph E. Green was the pastor. After his message, he invited anyone who wanted to receive the baptism of the Holy Spirit with the evidence of speaking in tongues to come down to the altar. I went down, and Bishop Green said, I am going to lay my hands on you, and all you have to do is open your mouth and speak. I was a little nervous, but when he put his hands on my forehead, I said, "Father, I receive your Spirit." I could feel the Holy Spirit rising. As I opened my mouth, I started speaking in tongues— a language other than my native language or any language known to me. I started crying and praising God. I felt like I did at Jericho Baptist Church that first night. I realized then that it is easy for anyone to receive. You can't speak in English and tongues at the same time. I had to yield my vocal cords to the Holy Spirit and allow Him to speak. I received my prayer language. If you believe, you can receive. Scripture tells us that whatever we ask in prayer, believing we can receive (Mark 11:24). I can use my prayer language at any time, and it is the best way to pray. When you pray in your prayer language, the enemy does not know what you are saying. It is a language that only God knows; it is from your spirit to His Spirit (Romans 8:26) or from your heart to His heart.

I felt so good. I came home and called my friend Helen and told her. (She had received a week earlier.) I began to see everything differently. The love of the Father became very real to me. I began to see the Scriptures differently; even John 3:16 was different to me. I knew that God loved me and that His Word was true. I told my family what had happened, but they didn't understand.

I went to work the next day, and I told Lillie Jackson what had happened to me. A couple of weeks earlier she told me at lunch that she had received the baptism of the Holy Spirit. I did not know her, and I was surprised when she stopped by my table in the cafeteria to say that to me. That was all she said. God always has a ram in the bush. Through Lillie, He confirmed to me that what I was asking God for was available to me.

My hunger to know God increased. I began to read Christian books and to study the Bible. I purchased Bible Study books and read at least one lesson every night before going to bed. I eventually enrolled in a Bible college. I enjoyed Bible College; I was excited about the Word.

For four years I attended Jericho Bible College. It was different being taught the Word instead of having the Word preached at me. Preaching often involved a pastor selecting a subject from part of the Scripture and presenting it. Teaching not only involves explanations and clarification, it includes providing the meaning of the Word and application for daily life. It makes a difference.

In my senior year at Jericho, I felt like I was not learning anything. We were studying the book of

Revelation. While we had a good teacher, I did not always understand her explanation of Scripture. While I kept that to myself, I finally tried to get a different explanation in class. Near the end of the last semester, in preparation for our final exams, the teacher reviewed all the material that she had taught us. There was one question that I could not answer. Instead of giving me the answer, she told me which chapter to read. I read the chapter but thought she should have given us the answer. I kept that thought to myself also. My sister Jewell, my friend Helen, and I went to Bible school together every week. We studied for the final exam together and at the end of the following week we took the exam. The exam was two hours long, and the question that the teacher did not answer was on the test. We all finished the exam around the same time, and we all had different answers to the question. When I walked out of the classroom, one of the other students asked me how I did. All I could say was that I did not know about one answer. I did the best I could. I laughed at his idea that I would be the class speaker. "Watch what I tell you," he said.

At the end of the school year, Jericho Bible College held a banquet for all the students. At the banquet, teachers announced the speakers for each class and distributed trophies to honor students. My teacher called several names but not mine. At the end of her presentation, she announced that I was the senior class speaker. Shocked I walked up to get my trophy. When I took it, she whispered in my ear, "You were the only one who got all the correct answers.". On the night of the final exam, I asked the Holy Spirt to give me what to write. He spoke to me, "You learned more than what you thought you did in this class."

The next year I went back and took the Old Testament Class, I started going to conferences to learn more about the Word. I went to Oklahoma, Pennsylvania, New York, New Jersey, North Carolina, South Carolina, Georgia, etc. My understanding and daily life changed. I applied the Word of God to every aspect of my life. Praise and worship, my authority as a believer, healing, and deliverance, all brought meaning to my life. It also gave me the opportunity to bless the lives of others.

My faith began to grow, and my prayer life changed. When I prayed, I expected God to answer. I expected to see the things about which I prayed. I saw things change in my family, at work and in the lives of my friends. I began each day with an hour in the morning and ended the day with an hour of prayer at night. I began to do what the Holy Spirit allowed me to see myself doing just as He revealed it.

I learned to pray Scriptures; I knew that if I prayed according to the Word, it resulted in an answer from God. I found new confidence in the Word. I prayed for healing for people; I visited the hospital and their homes. I boldly moved out to do whatever the Word committed or commissioned us to do. I was a new creature in Christ Jesus.

Lillie Jackson and I went to visit my cousin and his wife. I wanted to talk to them about the baptism of the Holy Spirit. I wanted everyone in my family to receive and experience the improved living and closeness to God that I enjoyed. We talked for a few minutes about the purpose of our visit. Responding to their interest in receiving the baptism of the Holy Spirit, we began to pray with them. Immediately, I saw myself praying for my cousin first. His wife was next to me, so I started praying for her instead. She did not receive or speak, so I finally did what I had seen myself doing. I went to my cousin and prayed. He received right away and spoke in tongues. Then I went back to his wife and, this time, I touched her while praying in tongues and she started speaking in tongues. I realized then; I should have done what the Holy Spirit had shown me. God has allowed me to pray for many people in my family, and they have received the baptism of the Holy Spirit, salvation, healing, and deliverance. God is so good.

The following Scriptures were the ones I read and meditated on to receive the baptism of the Holy Spirit:

And I will pray the Father, and He will give you another Helper, that He may abide with you forever (John 14: 16, 17).

44 While Peter was still speaking these words, the Holy Spirit fell upon all those who heard the word. 45 And those of the circumcision who believed were astonished, as many as came with Peter, because the gift of the Holy Spirit had been poured out on the Gentiles also. 46 For they heard them speak with tongues and magnify God (Acts 10:44-46).

If you then, being evil, know how to give good gifts to your children, how much more will your heavenly Father give the Holy Spirit to those who ask Him" (Luke 11:13)!

2 He said to them, "Did you receive the Holy Spirit when you believed?" So they said to him, "We have not so much as heard whether there is a Holy Spirit." 5 When they heard this, they were baptized in the name of the Lord Jesus.

6 And when Paul had laid hands on them, the Holy Spirit came upon them, and they spoke with tongues and prophesied (Acts 19: 2, 5, 6).

But you shall receive power when the Holy Spirit has come upon you... (Acts 1:8a).

2 For he who speaks in a tongue does not speak to men but to God, for no one understands him; however, in the spirit he speaks mysteries. 3 But he who prophesies speaks edification and exhortation and comfort to men. 4 He who speaks in a tongue edifies himself, but he who prophesies edifies the church. 5 I wish you all spoke with tongues, but even more that you prophesied; for he who prophesies is greater than he who speaks with tongues, unless indeed he interprets, that the church may receive edification. 6 But now, brethren, if I come to you speaking with tongues, what shall I profit you unless I speak to you either by revelation, by knowledge, by prophesying, or by teaching? 7 Even things without life, whether flute or harp, when they make a sound, unless they make a distinction in the sounds, how will it be known what is piped or played? 8 For if the trumpet makes an uncertain sound, who will prepare for battle? [9] So likewise you, unless you utter by the tongue words easy to understand, how will it be known what is spoken? For you will be speaking into the air. [10] There are, it may be, so many kinds of languages in the world, and none of them is without significance. [11] Therefore, if I do not know the meaning of the language, I shall be a foreigner to him who speaks, and he who speaks will be a foreigner to me. [12] Even so you, since you are zealous for spiritual gifts, let it be for the edification of the church that you seek to excel. [13] Therefore let him who speaks in a tongue pray that he may interpret.[14] For if I pray in a tongue, my spirit prays, but my understanding is unfruitful. [15] What is the conclusion then? I will pray with the spirit, and I will also pray with the understanding. I will sing with the spirit, and I will also sing with the understanding...[18] I thank my God I speak with tongues more than you all. [27] If anyone speaks in a tongue, let there be two or at the most three, each in turn, and let one interpret (1 Corinthians: 14:2-15, 18, 27).

And they were all filled with the Holy Spirit and began to speak with other tongues, as the Spirit gave them utterance (Acts 2:4).

...Praying always with all prayer and supplication in the Spirit, being watchful to this end with all perseverance and supplication for all the saints... (Ephesians 6:18).

Prayer

Pray this prayer if you want to receive the baptism of the Holy Spirit:

Jesus, I believe that you died on the cross for my sins and You were raised from the dead. I repent of my sin, and I ask You to forgive me for every word, action, or deed that I have done knowingly and unknowingly. I am Your child. Your Word says, "How much more will your heavenly Father give the Holy Spirit to those who ask." I ask You to fill me now with Your Spirit.

Thank You, Jesus, for filling me with Your Spirit. In Jesus' name, Amen.

(Take three deep breaths—breathe in and out three times. Open your mouth and allow the Holy Spirit to take control of your tongue. Start speaking in your heavenly language. Remember, you cannot speak in English and tongues at the same time.)

Ask the Holy Spirit to give you a hunger and thirst for the Word. Begin by reading every day and asking Him to give you a revelation of what you just read. Allow Him to take you through the Bible and any book that you read. I recommend that you write in a journal any revelation or thoughts you receive.

Before reading, reach out to God in Prayer:

"Father, help me to understand Your Word. Give me wisdom; show me how to apply Your Word to my life every day. In Jesus' name, Amen."

Include these Scriptures often in your study and meditation time:

Blessed are those who hunger and thirst for righteousness, for they shall be filled (Matthew 5:6, NIV).

Give me understanding, and I shall keep Your law; indeed, I shall observe it with my whole heart (Psalm 119:34, NIV).

Trust in the Lord with all your heart, and lean not on your own understanding; in all your ways acknowledge Him, and He shall direct your path (Proverbs 3:5, 6, NIV).

To do evil is like sport to a fool, but a man of understanding has wisdom (Proverbs 10:23).

For the Lord gives wisdom from His mouth comes knowledge and understanding (Proverbs 2:6, NIV).

Notes and Reflections

Under the Authority of the House

My mother was Baptist, and my father was Methodist. As children, we always attended church with my mother. I grew up Baptist and continued to observe Baptist teaching as an adult. All I knew was the Baptist denomination.

As my walk with the Father grew more intimate, He began to show me things in the Word. I began to visit other churches. I believed differently from what I learned in the Baptist church. I applied what I learned in my daily living, and I saw results in my life. I continued to see and know Jesus loves me and understand that His Word is true.

As I studied the Word, I was reminded that the Father sent Jesus to die for my sins. The Father wanted me delivered out of darkness into His marvelous light. I remember taking an accounting class for my job. I did not understand what formula to use to find the correct answer; however, I prayed and asked the Holy Spirit to help me to understand what to do, and He did. My final grade for the class was an "A." I know it was because of Him that I got that "A." There were times when I did not have money to pay a bill, but I prayed, and the Father always provided what I needed.

I prayed for people to receive healing and to receive the baptism of the Holy Spirit. I wanted everyone, especially my church friends, to receive the baptism of the Holy Spirit. I knew that the same love, joy, and peace that I experienced would also enrich their lives.

My friends and I prayed for the people at our church to receive the baptism of the Holy Spirit and that their lives would be changed. They experienced the joy, peace, and love of the Father, which they had never experienced before. They began to have a relationship with Him, rather than just knowing about Him. The Word became real to them, and they began to apply it to their everyday situations.

I prayed with others in the church that things would change at my church. We prayed for a revelation of the Father, and that the work of the Holy Spirit would be received and taught by church leadership. The more we prayed, the more things remained the same. One day I had a dream (or I received this during prayer, I can't remember) that a lot of people left the church and that my church started operating in the gifts of the Spirit. I shared with the others who prayed for a change in the church. The meaning of that dream/vision would soon be clear.

One Sunday after devotion was over, I got up and went out into the church foyer. I could not stay inside; I was very restless, and I did not know why. I stayed in the foyer until the message/preaching was over. The Junior Ushers served that day. Because I was one of the directors supervising them, I could not leave church while they were still on duty. As soon as the service was over I went home. I was still restless; I could not sleep or eat. I called my friend Dianne, but the phone just rang and rang—no answer. I thought maybe I should go out and get something to eat, so I asked my son to go with me. We got to the restaurant and ordered food, but I was unable to eat when the food came. We boxed it up and brought it home. Once I got home, I called Dianne again and this time, she answered. I told her I needed to talk to her and that I would be right down. She said okay, and I drove to her home in Clinton, Maryland.

Dianne invited me in and said, "Sis. Brenda, we could have talked on the phone. You did not have to come all the way down here this late at night." I told her I did not know why but I believed that I had to come to see her. I went straight to her basement and took a seat. Dianne remained upstairs. Finally, she came down and told me that the Holy Spirit had just spoken to her about why I was there. God is going to give you directions. We are going to pray, and you will know why you are here. We prayed, and she prophesied over me. The Holy Spirit said that He was drawing me out from the church. If I wanted to continue to grow and be used by God, I had to come out from under the authority of my then current church. Father God does not create conflicts of authority within His house. I accepted the Father's plan and told the Holy Spirit that moment that I would not return to that church anymore. (I cried like a baby, and when I finished crying I was at peace.) Release from anxiety and restlessness followed those words that brought me into an agreement with the Father's will. I had never experienced such confidence. My peace and joy were restored.

The next day I called the president of the Usher Board and told her that I would not be back and that I would no longer be over the Junior Ushers. I explained to her that after seventeen or eighteen years it was time for me to leave. I knew just about everybody there; my kids were involved there, but I wanted to be obedient. (I had already given up the other positions that I held in the church.) Serving with the ushers was the only thing holding me there. I had a lot of friends on the Usher Board, but I was determined to do what God said.

My sister Jewell was a member there also; I called her and told her I was not coming back. She asked me whether I was sure that I was doing the right thing; I told her that I was certain. I called Helen and told her I was leaving. She accepted my decision and shared that she was praying asking God whether she should leave also. Many others left the church in response to the Holy Spirit's direction in their individual lives. When any person follows the leading of God, the peace of God follows. I experienced that peace.

On Sundays, I prayed to find the church where the Father desired to plant me. I visited approximately four or five other churches. I was led to a church where believers accepted and sought the gifts of the Spirit. I witnessed a lot of miracles at this church, and I became a member. There is freedom and renewed purpose when we obey the Father and submit to leadership that He has assigned to teach and care for you. When I entered the doors of my new church, I experienced that freedom and excitement. A new level of growth in the Father began. I trusted the Father. I knew it was the right place.

The pastor had a heart of compassion for the people and ministered to them with the heart of Jesus. He wanted everyone healed, delivered, and set free. He taught on healing and deliverance. Some Sundays, he would pray for everyone in the church and people would be delivered and healed. His countenance would change when he began to flow in the spirit. I knew when I arrived that my time there would be short. The assignment was to sit, listen, and observe. That is exactly what I did. I was there for four years.

During that time, the anointing on my life increased tremendously. The presence and power of God were physically evident as I allowed Him to use me to reach and serve His people. (My hand would get hot when I prayed for people.) God began to use me for deliverance, healing, and praying for people to receive the baptism of the Holy Spirit. I know I cannot do anything without God the Father and that He is the one that is doing the work. He (the Holy Spirit) gave me the Words, opportunity, and timing to act and people were set free.

At our family reunion that year, we were getting ready to close the business part of our gathering, and they asked me to pray for the family. I asked everyone to join hands and for those who wanted healing to come to the middle of the circle. I began to pray, and all at once the presence of God just hovered over us. The Holy Spirit led me to call for legions of warring angels to come and help me fight in this spiritual battle for the lives gathered. The atmosphere changed at that moment. People began to weep before God; some shouted, and some could not remain standing in God's presence. It was awesome; God did work in my family that day, and He is still working.

Later on that week, my cousin called me and asked me to come to her family's house and have prayer with them. My sister Janet went with me. When we arrived, they were all outside on the porch. We began to talk about the salvation Scriptures. I shared about the baptism of the Holy Spirit, and I asked whether they wanted to receive. They all said yes. I prayed for each one of them, and they all received with the evidence of speaking in tongues. My cousin's husband was mowing the grass while we were praying. She said that she wanted her husband to receive also, and she went and got him. We prayed, and he received. We praised God, and we went home.

On one of my visits home to Georgia, a lady I was very close to wanted me to come and pray for her and her children. I said okay. My sisters, Jewell and Effie, and I went to her house to pray for all of them to be delivered. I don't think I had ever prayed for an entire family to be delivered. When we got there, we talked for a few minutes and then we started to pray. Everyone in her family got in a circle. There were five of them, and I was in the middle of the circle. I began to pray in tongues. I could sense the forces that were there. As I prayed, I laid hands on one child and cast a spirit out. The evicted spirit entered the next person. As I moved from one to another, the spirit moved to the next person until I got to the mother. She was to be the last to receive prayer. My sister Effie noticed how the mother's facial expression changed. Each time a child was prayed for, the mother's expression changed. Well, when I laid hands on her, her face became distorted, her eyes were blood red, and she fell back on the sofa. The spirit left, and her face and eyes became normal again. Praise God, He is a deliverer. We all began to praise God for setting them free.

When we got home, we were in the kitchen talking about how Father God had set them free. My sister Effie said, "I have never seen anything like that before. All I could do was pray." My sister Jewell agreed that she, too, only could pray. My sister Effie looked at Jewell with a surprised look on her face and said, "I thought that was why you came with Brenda—because you knew what to do." I told both of them that they did the right thing by praying. Prayer was what was needed. We all laughed and praised God for what He had done in that family.

On another occasion, my sister-in-law Clara said that the doctor had diagnosed her with breast cancer, and she came to the house for prayer. We praised God, and as the presence of the Holy Spirit manifested in the room, I laid hands on her and commanded the spirit of cancer to come out of her. She gagged as if she was choking. Then she spat up this ugly looking dark substance and began to praise God. She said she knew that was the cancer. She went back to the doctor, and they could not find any cancer in her body. I shared with my family how they needed to confess the Word about healing daily and to study the Word. It was important to pray and offer God praise and worship. I encouraged them to ask the Holy Spirit to give them revelation of the Word and to show them how to apply it to their lives.

I prayed for my uncle, and he was filled with the Holy Spirit and delivered from demonic oppression. I went to my cousin's house, and she had at lead ten members of the family there. God filled all of them with the Holy Spirit with the evidence of speaking in tongues. Later my sister-in-law, Alberta, received the Holy Spirit. Alberta had been diagnosed with Lupus, so I prayed for her healing. She had been taking medication for Lupus for a long time. The side effects of the medication had caused other health problems. She had to have most of her intestines removed. We went to see her in the hospital in Atlanta, Georgia, after the surgery. We all waited in her room and prayed during the surgery. When she returned to the room, she said she felt like she needed to have a bowel movement. The nurses said that was impossible, but she kept asking for a bed pan. Finally, one of the nurses gave her a bed pan just to prove that she did not need it. Well, she did need it. The nurses were wrong.

She remained in the hospital for a long time. The doctors told my brother James that she was not going to make it. Alberta probably would not live through the night. We prayed, and she made it through the night. A month later they said the same thing. We continued to pray, and she lived. They finally stopped saying that she was dying and admitted that they did not know what was happening. She lived at least three or four months after the doctors said she was not going to make it through the night. I believe she decided to go and not fight anymore. I will always have fond memories of her. She believed, and she received so easily.

Most of the times when I went to Georgia, family members, and others, would come to my mother's house for me to pray with them or for them. One day my nephew brought his friends to see me, and they wanted prayer. I had just gotten home from church, and I had not eaten anything, so I prayed for them. God set them free from demonic oppression and when they left someone else came, and I prayed for them. It seemed like that day people were coming from every-where for prayer. I did not get to eat until later that evening because I would not eat if I were going to pray for someone. I wanted God to use me. I wanted everyone to be healed, delivered, and set free. I made a special trip to Georgia to pray for salvation for all my brothers. At that time, I had four brothers. All of them received salvation, and three of them received the baptism of the Holy Spirit.

Through it all, I learned that it makes a difference who you are sitting under and what you are hearing. You are blessed when sitting under a pastor who is a worshiper with a good prayer life. The anointing that fuels the pastor's ministry is available to those in the congregation who, like the pastor, enjoy a relationship with the Holy Spirit, and live by the revealed Word of God. The growth and development of the congregation are well connected to the pastor's knowledge, revelation, and submission to God. What the leadership has will be taught to the congregation. God is a person of order. He will place you in the right place to learn and receive from Him. This is another benefit of walking with the Father. Let Him do all the leading and you need only follow Him.

Prayer

Father, I thank You today for all that You have taught me and are still teaching me. I want to be all You created me to be. I want to fulfill my purpose. I am open to receive from You. Create in me a clean heart, and renew the right spirit within me. I yield myself to You. In Jesus' name, Amen.

Behold how good and how pleasant it is for brethren to dwell together in unity. It is like the precious oil upon the head; running down on the beard, the beard of Aaron, running down on the edge of his garments (Psalm 133: 1-2).

The steps of a good man are ordered by the Lord. And He delights in his ways; though he falls, he shall not be utterly cast down. For the Lord upholds him with His hands (Psalm 37:23).

Father, I ask You to guide

_____

as they seek Your directions for their life. Order their steps today, give them wisdom and under- standing, and continue to draw them to You. In Jesus' name, Amen.

Notes and Reflections

My Walk into Forgiveness

The more I read and studied the Word of God, the more I began to know Him. The more I learned about God's character, the more I learned about myself. I saw my shortcomings and the person I could become, the person God sees when He looks at me, thinks of me. The Word showed me what I was not and who I should become. Every day as I read the Word I asked for understanding and wisdom to apply it to my life.

One day during my prayer time, as I was praying the Holy Spirit showed me that I needed to go to my father and ask for forgiveness. When I heard that in my spirit, I had to think really about that. I did not think that I had done anything to my father that warranted a request for forgiveness. If anything, he should have been asking me for forgiveness.

My father was an alcoholic. Because he was drunk most weekends, he never took us anywhere, and I never wanted him to take me anyplace. We lived in the country and the only time we went somewhere was on the weekend. My sister Effie and I were in a Bible study group. Each family hosted meetings on a rotating basis. We never wanted our turn to host to come. I feared my father would come home drunk during the Bible study. Well, guess what, when it was our turn to hold the study at our house, he came home drunk. He said something that embarrassed me, but the teacher didn't seem to mind. I did.

All those memories went through my mind, and I said out loud, "Okay God. If you want me to go home and ask for forgiveness, I will." About a month later, I went home and waited until late at night to speak with my father. He and I were the only ones in the room. I shared with him what the Holy Spirit had spoken to me about asking him for forgiveness. I asked him to forgive me for anything that I had ever said or done to him. I explained that I never intended to hurt him and that if I did, I was sorry. Once I said that I felt really good; I felt a release. My father said, "That's okay baby" and he left the room. I was waiting for him to apologize to me but he didn't. It was not about him saying anything to me. It was about me being obedient to the Holy Spirit. After he had left the room, I laughed to myself and said, "That was funny." I knew I had done what God wanted me to do.

After that, I began to lay hands on people that had more complicated problems. I prayed that God would heal the emotional or spiritual wound feeding a continuing source of doubt, worry, and unbelief. Such people experience difficulty in daily life and challenge in their growth as Christians. God answered those prayers. I saw Him set people free from demonic oppression. I experienced increased boldness and confidence in every assignment that God gave me. I continued to pray for people to receive the baptism of the Holy Spirit and they would receive and begin to speak in tongues immediately. Everything for me went to another level. Later, my father allowed me to pray for him. He recommitted his life to Christ (praise God) and we became friends. I called him, and we had some wonderful conversations. He would even give me advice on how to minister to some people.

My dad was a good man. His past life experiences contributed to his struggles with alcohol. However, when he rededicated his life to Christ, he changed. He was not perfect, but I know God continued working on him, just as He continues to work on me.

One Sunday after church, a woman asked for prayer and two other people joined me to pray for her. During the time we were praying the Holy Spirit brought this Scripture to my mind: *If you don't forgive men their sins, your Father will not forgive your sins* (Matthew 6:14, NIV). After we had finished praying, I asked her if she had any unforgiveness against anyone. I shared the Scripture that I had received, but she said that she just could not forgive her brother for what he had done to her. I told her that if she did not forgive her brother, God would not be able to forgive her. She said, "I can't forgive him" and left the church. She did not want to hear anything else. After she had left, I prayed that the Holy Spirit would show her that she needed to forgive her brother and that He would show her how to forgive.

I know that deep wounds sometimes prevent people from discussing hurts that people have caused them in the past. If you live with that kind of pain, ask the Father to help you forgive the person who caused it. Forgiveness is a process, and the Father can and is willing to help you. Unforgiveness is an open door to sickness and disease. It is a door that the enemy will use against you. Ask the Father to show you what is in your heart that blocks your blessings, healing, or a closer relationship with Him. If there is any unforgiveness, release it to God today. Don't hold on to it, release it to Him.

I purpose in my heart every day to walk in forgiveness, and I ask the Father to help me. It is a daily walk with the Father that will keep you on the right path. As you journey with Him, He will speak to you about those things in your heart that are not like Him. The moment you realize what it is, release it immediately to Him. He is a good Father, and He wants all of His children to walk in forgiveness.

My Prayer Suggestion for You

Father, You know my heart better than I do. Show me those things that are not right. I want to walk in forgiveness. I do not want to hold on to anything any longer that will hinder my relationship with You. Please forgive me for holding on to things that happened in the past. I release them to You now; and if I have any unforgiveness in my heart show me and I will, with Your help, forgive and release them. In Jesus' name, I pray, Amen.

For if you forgive men their trespasses, your heavenly Father will also forgive you. But if you do not forgive men their trespasses, neither will your Father forgive your trespasses (Matthew 6:14-15).

For with what judgment you judge, you will be judged; and with the measure you use, it will be measured back to you (Matthew 7:2).

And whenever you stand praying, if you have anything against anyone, forgive him that your Father in heaven may also forgive you your trespasses. But if you do not forgive, neither will your Father in heaven forgive your trespasses (Mark 11:25-26).

Intimate Relationship

One day I decided to take my Father by the hand and allow Him to lead me all day, twenty-four hours. That day I realized that He is with me every day. (It is a choice that I make each day.) His word says that He will never leave me nor forsake me. That promise keeps the Father intimately involved in all that is important in my life. Even before making that choice, I started my day off with prayer and reading the Scriptures. I normally did that every morning. But the day I decided to seek a more intimate relationship with the Father, I prayed for my family, and this Scripture came into my mind: *"Believe in the Lord Jesus Christ and thou shall be saved and thy house"* (Acts 16:31).

I read it and got up off my knees and started out of the room in my house where I go to pray and do Bible study (my prayer room). I heard this voice in my spirit say, "You don't know what the house is, do you?" Startled, I answered, "No I don't." In a vision, the Holy Spirit showed me a church with the top lifted off, with all the different families sitting in the pews. The Holy Spirit said, "See all the families here? They do not all live in one physical house, but they are all in the house of the Lord." Immediately I saw the house of Jacob's household. I saw the tents they inhabited. They were in one big tent and a lot of smaller tents. I realized that my entire family was in my house, and they were all saved. I rejoiced all day over what He had shown me from that one Scripture.

I praised God all the way to work (I worked for a bank, and I was the manager of the Home Equity Department). Once I got there, I asked the Holy Spirit to help me get everything completed promptly (Proverbs 3: 5-6). That day, I was able to get everything completed that I needed to do. That very seldom happened in the past (James 1:5). I realized that no aspect of my daily activity escaped the Fathers attention and provision.

I talked to my friend, Lillie Jackson, at work that day. I shared with her what the Holy Spirit had spoken to me that morning before I left home. Excited by the Holy Spirit's revelation, she agreed with me that every member of my family would be saved.

My trip home from work that day was still happy and full of praise for God. My joy was so full that I sensed the very presence of God. It was as if He was sitting there in the car with me. Have you ever sensed that someone is behind you? The Father's presence in the car was so powerful that I looked up in my mirror to see if I could see Him. Since that revelation, I have stood in the gap and prayed the Father's resolution for any and every family need. When you stand in the gap for your family, you are taking their place, interceding for them until there is a change or resolution to the problem.

At times, I prayed in tongues or English, whatever the Holy Spirit directed me to say. I prayed for an hour for my family every night before bed. Once a week my friend Helen joined me at home in prayer for our families. Janice, another friend, would come on a different night during the week to pray for our families. We always made a list and prayed over their names. Sometimes we touched the names with oil. We invited the Holy Spirit to manifest Himself to them, and I believed that anything hindering them would be broken from their lives.

I began to make trips to Georgia to talk to family members. In those early talks with them, it was clear that they did not understand. One of my sisters asked me how I knew that she did not have the Holy Spirit, just as I did. I knew she would have told me if she had already received. During a phone conversation with my mother, she said that she did not understand and was not sure whether she wanted to receive. Everyone in your family is not going to support you all of the time. You may experience opposition from those closest to you. It is important to know within yourself what is right. God will reveal and confirm it and resolve any conflict.

Shortly after the conversation with my mother, I went home to Georgia. When I got there, I did not say anything about the baptism of the Holy Spirit to my mother. I noticed that she kept looking at me, and I went out on the porch to read. She came outside where I was and said, "Brenda, you are different, you don't look the same." She said that she could tell there was a difference in me. I shared about the baptism of the Holy Spirit, how I felt about the Word, and how I know that Jesus loves me.

Later that day my sister Effie who lived in South Carolina and my sister-in-law Clara came to the house. When I shared with them and asked whether they would like to receive the baptism of the Holy Spirit, they both said yes. We went into one of the bedrooms and began to pray. I asked God to fill them with His Spirit, and He did. They both received and spoke in tongues. I asked my mother if she wanted to receive and she hesitated. "Come on mother let her pray for you," my sister said.

I prayed for her, but she did not receive. She left the bedroom. The next morning, I went back to Maryland. A couple of months later, I went back to Georgia to visit my parents. My mother asked me to pray for her to receive the baptism of the Holy Spirit. She told me that she had seen Jesus standing before her with outstretched hands to her when I last prayed that she receives. She walked away from Him and was so sorry that she did. I agreed to pray for her and continued to go about my day. When my mother came to me again, she asked when I would pray. I told her that I would pray for her as soon as my sister came over. When my sister arrived, we went into the same bedroom as before to pray. As soon as I opened my mouth to pray, my mother began to speak in tongues before I even touched her. Praise God, she had already received. She only needed to be encouraged to open her mouth and allow the language to come forth.

My sister Janet, who lived in Indiana, also disagreed with my decision to receive the baptism of the Holy Spirit. She was in a traditional church at the time. I remember one time we were visiting my parents at the same time. For every word I said, my sister had something different to say. It did not matter what we were talking about; she disagreed. I left the room instead of arguing with her, and she followed me wherever I went. Finally, later that night, I asked her if I could pray with her. She said, "NO, I don't want you to pray for me." I said okay and went to bed. I prayed and asked the Father what was going on. I knew she needed to be delivered, but she permitted the enemy to use her. I was angry with the spirit that controlled her. Just as I finished praying, she came into my room and said, "Brenda, I'm sorry. Yes, I want you to pray for me." I jumped out of bed and prayed. The Father set her free, and she received the baptism of the Holy Spirit with the evidence of speaking in tongues. I thank God for setting her free. God is so faithful.

God is so good. I saw a lot of my family accept Jesus Christ into their hearts and be filled with the baptism of the Holy Spirit. I believe that the baptism of the Holy Spirit is important for every believer, to have that power of God working in their lives (Acts 1:8). God has performed many miracles in my family and for people in my hometown. According to their need, some were saved; others were healed, delivered, and set free all by the power of God.

I had to be persistent and consistent with praise and worship, and prayer. The Word of God, reading, praying, and thinking about the Word became a priority in my daily life. I continued to have a set time to pray every morning and evening. The result of that prayer brought unexpected outcomes.

One morning, having exceeding my usual prayer time, I rushed to get dressed for work. I did not like to be late for work; in fact, most of the time, I was early. I liked to get to work, get my desk set up, and relax a few minutes before I started dealing with the customers. On this particular day, I rushed out to my car and started up the street. I heard a loud voice insist, "Slow down! That man is going to walk in front of your car." Immediately, I hit the brakes and then looked to the left. There was a man stepping off the curb in the middle of traffic. My car didn't hit him, but he walked to my car and fell. Getting up, he looked at me and picked up his backpack. Without saying a word, he walked in front of my car, crossed the street, and got on the bus. I was so shocked that I could not move; I just sat there while the cars behind me started to blow their horns for me to move. I was shaking like a leaf on a tree. I could not believe what had just happened. I had to pull off to the side of the street and get myself together.

The enemy accused me of hitting the man, insisting that he would die later. The Holy Spirit reminded me that I had seen the man, uninjured, stand and walk away. I praised God all the way to work. God is so good, and He is faithful. In each life given to Him, He watches over His Word to perform it. The Holy Spirit spoke very loudly to me that day to prevent hurt and protect me from all harm, even from falling into the trap of the enemy. What the devil means for harm, God can turn it into good. I now ask the Holy Spirit to lead me every day and to guide my steps.

In addition to showing me about my family and other concerns, the Holy Spirit has shown me about work also. As a loan officer, I prepared the paperwork needed to process an equity line of credit for a customer. In a specific case, the Holy Spirit told me to look at the instructions for the title company when I got to work. When I reviewed the documents, I saw a mistake that I had made. I was able to correct that mistake before the paperwork was sent to closing. The Holy Spirit has helped me on every job that I have had. He continues to help me now that I am retired.

Why don't you allow Him to take you by the hand and lead you 24 hours? You will be amazed at what you will hear and see. He is waiting. Make that decision now. Ask the Father to lead you today. He is waiting with his hands extended to you. Come, allow Jesus to be Lord of your life. He is willing to lead and guide you every step of the way.

When you pray or worship God, always take a pad and pen with you. When you finish, wait a few minutes in His presence and write down every thought that comes into your mind. You will begin to hear and understand more as the Holy Spirit talks to you about all the concerns you share in prayer, all the concerns of your heart.

When we acknowledge the Father, He will direct our paths. While taking a shower one morning, I received guidance on a trip my husband planned to take. He had planned to drive to Georgia to see his family, but I had planned to stay at home. I just thought it would be a good time to be home by myself. The moment I turned the water on the Holy Spirit spoke to me about the trip. He encouraged me to go with my husband to Georgia. I cried and said okay. I was selfish thinking only of myself by planning to stay at home.

During visits to Georgia, we always visited with my family first and then my husband's mother. When we got to his mother's house, I knew why I was supposed to visit her. In talking with her, I found out that the doctor thought she had bone cancer. I prayed for her healing, and I felt in my spirit that she was healed when we prayed. She looked better before I left that day and she said she felt better too. When she went back to the doctor for follow-up, he could not find any cancer in her body. Since then I always go with my husband when he wants to go back to Georgia for a visit.

I learned that each person's need and circumstances require specific direction from the Holy Spirit. Often, I have prayed for other people who I knew in the church and my neighborhood. When I have gone out to pray, in private homes and especially when visiting in the hospital, another person has accompanied me. Before entering a home, the Holy Spirit said, "Apply the blood of Jesus over you before you go into this house." I stopped immediately and prayed as directed. Once inside, I could sense a lot of things going on. I prayed and left; however, I did return at a later date with a friend who agreed with me in prayer. God moved in that situation setting her free from depression.

Below is a list of some of the Scriptures that I prayed and stood on for the salvation of my family:

... Believe on the Lord Jesus Christ and you will be saved, you and your household (Acts 16:31).

For God so loved the world that He gave His only begotten Son, that whoever believes in Him should not perish but have everlasting life (John 3:16).

For the Son of Man has come to seek and to save that which was lost (Luke 19:10).

Assuredly, I say to you, whatever you bind on earth will be bound in heaven, and whatever you loose on earth will be loosed in heaven (Matthew 18:18).

Therefore pray the Lord of the harvest to send out laborers into His harvest (Matthew 9:38).

My Prayer for You

Father, I thank you for the person reading this book, and I ask you to give them wisdom and revelation knowledge of your Word. I pray that they will allow You to lead them for 24 hours and that their lives will never be the same. Holy Spirit, teach them how to stand in the gap for their family and how to be consistent and persistent with praise and worship, prayer, and studying the Word. In Jesus' name, Amen.

Notes and Reflections

A Walk into Balance

I believe the Father has brought me to a place of "Balance" in my life. In my earlier years, when I started my journey, my life was out of balance. The Father, Son, and Holy Spirit have gently nudged me into a place of balance.

I was a person who thought, "I have a brain, and I can make decisions without asking God. He is not concerned with the little things that are going on in my life." The amount of time I spent with my family did not matter, as long as I cooked and kept the house clean. As long as I was doing something good for God, I thought everything else was alright. How I handled my finances, where my kids went to school, etc. were all my responsibilities. I forgot the Scripture that says, *"Trust in the Lord with all your heart, and lean not on your own understanding; in all your ways acknowledge Him, and He shall direct your path"* (Proverbs 3: 4-6).

I never consulted the Father about what I wanted to do. If I wanted to do it, I did. I did not include Him in my decisions. I only asked Him if I could not figure out what to do. But as the Father's love nudged me into a closer relationship with Him, all I wanted to do was please Him. That meant not my will, but the Father's will be done in my life. I gradually released my life to Him. The more I came to know about Him, the more I trusted Him. I wanted Him to talk to me every day in every circumstance and to tell me what to do.

Now I acknowledge Him early every morning and ask the Father to direct my footsteps. If I have a financial need that day, I ask Him, and He always supplies. Whatever the need is, He graciously supplies. I call Him my Friend and I talk to Him as my friend. When I receive an answer to something that I asked about or was praying about, I acted on it right away. It took me some time to realize that everything He showed me was not for that moment. I had to wait for the right time on some things. Now when I receive directions, I have learned to ask when to move or speak. I have learned to sit, wait, and listen carefully before acting on what I have heard. Sometimes I meditate on it a couple of days before acting on it. Gradually He brought about a balance in my life.

My personal obedience in everything became the response to every life activity. That included shopping, being the mother and wife, etc. I needed to acknowledge Him in everything. I began to share how I felt about the people in my life, church, and work. I became open and honest with my feelings. I told Him about things that I liked and disliked.

I am married with two adult children, one granddaughter, and one great-grandson. One night as I was praying the Holy Spirit spoke to me and said, "You need to spend more time with your husband and children." I heard Him loud and clear. When I heard that, I felt sad because I did not see their need. To me, everything seemed fine. I guess my eyes were closed to what was happening in my household.

I was a working mother, very active in my church and president of a women's ministry called Women in Fellowship, Inc. As I stated earlier, I was so excited about my relationship with the Father that I would read the Word and pray for an hour in the morning and an hour at night. Sometimes I would go into my prayer room to read or do Bible study and lose track of time. I would spend three to four hours with the Father. My husband would be asleep by the time I went to bed. He would make sure the kids were in bed and the next day, before he could get up, I had read and prayed before departing for work.

My husband is a good man, a hard worker and a good provider for his family. He always helped me with the children when they were young. He always dropped them off at the day care or school before He went to work and I picked them up in the evening. He never complained about me not spending time with him in the evenings. I guess that was why I was surprised when the Holy Spirit corrected me.

Change required trusting God. I began to pray for our marriage. Every night I prayed that I would be the wife my husband needed, and he would be the husband that I needed. God began to work on my heart, and our relationship grew closer. I adjusted what I was doing in the evenings when I got home from work. I started spending more time with my kids. We did things together on the weekends.

During the week, by the time they finished their homework, it was time for bed. I always made sure I talked to them about school and their friends. When my husband was ready to go to bed, I was ready also. Sometimes I would just go and sit with him and watch television, even though sometimes I did not want to watch what he was watching. I watched the programs he selected anyway. I started doing things with the kids also. I prayed for them in a way that I never had before. I began to see things that I did not like, and I started thinking about how I could help them have a relationship with the Father. I prayed about the things that I observed, like attitude and rebellion. I began to think about starting a fellowship meeting for children.

I talked with my friends at work and asked them what they thought of us getting together and having a children's fellowship once a month. We all agreed we would have the fellowship at my house monthly on the fourth Saturdays, and that I would serve refreshments for the kids. I worked at that time at American Security Bank. We prayed together every day at lunch time. We would meet in the basement of the bank and pray for thirty to forty minutes. We decided that day that Lillie Jackson and I would teach the older kids twelve and older; Mary Jordan and Kathleen Johnston would teach the kids ages eight to eleven, and Rachel Prince would teach the kids under eight. (I might have the age limit wrong, but this is how I remember it). The parents of the children would pray the entire time that we were teaching. Everyone had a separate room to teach the children.

I guess we had about 10-15 children attend the fellowship on a consistent basis every month. It was a wonderful fellowship for the children. Lillie and I would pray and ask the Holy Spirit what we should talk; we taught whatever He told us to teach. It would all come together when we met. We always had a time of teaching and after that, we would give the children an opportunity to talk and ask questions that they might have about anything.

The most important thing for the kids was that we promised them that we would not tell their parents what they had told us. We never betrayed their confidence or undermined the ability of each family to function independently. Parental authority was respected. The kids in the group never repeated anything that we discussed in those groups. My kids were in the group that I co-taught. They talked about me just like I was not sitting there and I did not say a word. But oh I knew how to pray and what to pray about!

We discussed prayer, salvation, faith, and having a relationship with the Father. From time to time, we would bring in other people to talk to the teens. One time we brought in Derek McCoy and Timothy Jackson from Hope Christian Church to talk to them about prom night. None of the parents, or teachers, were allowed in that meeting. The kids asked anything they wanted to know related to prom night. That included but was not limited to, what to expect, and how to make the right choices. On other occasions, Lillie's brother talked to the children. They seemed to connect with him.

I believe the Children's Fellowship was a great thing at the time for our children. They were taught things that they were not learning at church. The bonding that took place in the children was awesome; they grew comfortable with openness and enjoyed the opportunity to share with one another. They felt the liberty to be open with one another and to trust one another and to seek spiritual guidance from the adults at any time. We also taught the children the importance of prayer and how to receive from God.

If you ask God for something and believe when you ask, He will give it to you. Well, my son, Willie Jr. asked Lillie to pray with him for a computer (at the time they had just started teaching the kids how to use a computer). She prayed with him, and I said to myself, "I am not going to get him a computer. I don't have the money." He believed God heard his prayer. Well, as time went on, I don't know how it happened, I went to Circuit City and bought him a computer. On my way home from the store, I remembered what I said, and I began to laugh. I thought to myself, "God you are funny. You made the financial provision and led me to buy the computer I had not planned to get." Who can resist God or alter what He wills?

Prayer always brings more than what we ask. God's will for us always exceeds what we think or ask. Willie's faith began to grow because God had answered his prayer. He even began to hear God's voice for himself. On another occasion, he had missed the bus to come home from school. We live in the Suitland, Maryland, area, and he was going to a Christian school in Camp Springs, Maryland. He decided he was going to walk home from school. He started walking up the driveway from school and heard this voice say, "Go to the principal's office." Immediately he turned around and went back to school to the principal's office and told them that he missed the bus.

The principal called me, explained what had happened, and asked me to come and pick him up. When I got there, he got in the car and shared his experience. He told me what he heard and how he obeyed the voice. He went back to the school. I explained that it was dangerous for him to try to walk home from school and that it was too far for him to walk. Willie trusted and relied on the Father. He developed a relationship with the Father for himself.

The children's fellowship helped me to see what they needed and what was missing in our relationship. It helped me to bring balance in our home *concerning my children. I did not realize it at the time, but it became* clearer with the passage of time and learning how the Father interacts with us. In my opinion, my job as a mother became easier (smile.)

My daughter Tracie and I seemed at times to be at odds with each other. She was rebellious, and God began to show me how to pray for her. The church I left was also her church. While I initially permitted her to continue attending services at the church, I eventually caused her to join me at the new church. She was very upset because she was a member and served in their youth choir. She was baptized there and had friends there. When I realized that she needed to be taught as I was being taught, I told her she was going to join me at the church I was attending.

Tracie had an encounter with the Holy Spirit shortly after joining me at my church. God overshadowed her with his love and power. She shouted all over the pews, and when we got home, she was still rejoicing. The next day she was in the shower, and I guess she was talking to God. I heard all this noise coming from the bathroom; she was shouting in the shower. God is good, her attitude began to change. My children know how to pray and talk to God if they don't know anything else. They know the Father's love for them is real. He allowed Jesus, His Son to die on the cross for their sins and to rise victoriously from the dead. He filled them with the Holy Spirit, the power that they need to live a victorious life.

During this time, I was only involved in one ministry at church, but I attended Bible College at Jericho Baptist Church (now Jericho City of Praise). I went to Bible College one night a week, but it required a lot of time studying and completing homework. God began to gently show me how to bring it all into balance. I learned to acknowledge, consider, and ask Him every day what to do and how to do it.

Sometimes we can get caught up in doing what we believe to be good things. However, if it is not what God would have us do, the will of God is left undone. There is no substitute for obeying God. There is no reason to pick the good thing because He will lead us to His will in the end. The good things substituted for the will of God will be of no value. In the end, the substitute will burn like dross because God's choice is overlooked.

I remember one Sunday I had taken a friend to church with me. She lived in another part of the city. I drove past my church to pick her up and come back to my church, at least, thirty minutes one way beyond the church. I wanted her to come, so I picked her up every Sunday. One Sunday, when I was praying before going to pick her up, the Holy Spirit said, "Stay home and pray." I told the Holy Spirit that I could not stay home. I promised Burdetta that I would pick her up for communion. He said, "Call her. If she wants to go, she will." I reluctantly called her and said that I was not coming to get her. I was staying home. She said, "Okay Ms. Brenda, it's fine."

I began to intercede, and I prayed for what seemed like a long time. I don't remember how long it took, but it was deep intercession. Finally, I began to get a release in my spirit. My concern subsided, and I began to thank God and rejoice. While I didn't know who I was praying for at the time, the next day my sister Effie Whitner called. She told me that my mother had a slight stroke and that she was fine. I believe that I was interceding for my mother. I was so glad I stayed home and prayed. After that, I try always to acknowledge God and do what He says to do in every situation. I am not always obedient, but I do better than I once did. I am still growing and learning about my wonderful Father and Friend.

There is a natural order to everything in life. God is always first, the family is second, and the Church is third. As you acknowledge Him, He will direct your path. The key to balance is acknowledging Him every day in every situation and being obedient.

Are you out of "balance"?

Prayer

Father, I pray that You will open the eyes of the person that is reading this book. Allow them to see if they are out of balance in life. Show them where they are in every area of their lives. Father, You said in your Word if we acknowledge You, You would direct our paths and that the steps of a good man are ordered by the Lord. So we thank You for ordering our steps every day. Thank You for opening the eyes of our understanding and giving us the wisdom to be balanced and to maintain our balance. In Jesus' name, Amen.

My Walk as a Mentor

I am President of Women in Fellowship, Inc. (WIF). Our **mission** is to be an extension of the arm of God, showing love to women of every color and every nation. We are women called by God, who will work with people in and outside of their local churches, helping them to become whole, delivered, and set free. We are a mentoring organization. Our **purpose** is to help others have a closer relationship with Jesus Christ and establish a firm foundation in the Word of God.

WIF meets monthly at my home on the first Saturday of every month at 10:00 A.M. When we first organized in 1996, I made a covenant with God that I would have the meetings at my house if He would show up at the meetings. He has always kept His part of the agreement, and I have kept my part. I very seldom cancel a meeting because of the agreement we have. We are currently looking for a place to have our meetings and a place for our headquarters. We have grown, and I don't have enough room for everyone. However, the women don't seem to mind sitting close to each other so everyone can have a seat.

I always pray for the members of the ministry. Once I asked the Holy Spirit to show me how to help Joyce. Joyce seemed to be very shy. She never had much to say, and it appeared that she had difficulty making decisions. Before she joined WIF, we had met at Hope Christian Church in College Park, Maryland. We both were ushers and members of the same LifeNet group, a small group fellowship supporting relationship building with God and among the members of the congregation. When you became a member of Hope Christian Church, you were asked to join a LifeNet group. On the fourth Sunday of every month after service, everyone would meet at their LifeNet leader's house for fellowship and teaching. I enjoyed LifeNet.

As I prayed for Joyce, I realized that God wanted me to mentor her. I did not know what she was going to say, but I believed that was what the Holy Spirit was leading me to do. I called her and asked her if I could be her mentor. She thought about it and finally said yes. I was happy. I knew it was going to be interesting. I had never mentored anyone before. I told her I wanted to help her with praying and reading the Word. She had received the baptism of the Holy Spirit with the evidence of speaking in tongues at our LifeNet meeting.

I explained that I would call her every night except Saturday. (On Saturday night I would prepare my dinner for Sunday, I hate to come home from church on Sunday and cook dinner.) I would call her around 8 P.M., and we would pray and read the Word until 9 P.M. or later. We always prayed for one hour. I would pray before I called her and ask the Holy Spirit what Scripture we should read or what we should talk about. Sometimes I would just listen.

Listening to a person talk can tell you more about their spiritual need or level of development. In the beginning, I would call her, and I could tell by the way she answered the phone that she did not want to talk to me. There were times when I knew that she was distracted or watching television. I encouraged her to go into another room so that we could talk and pray. When she did that, everything changed. I asked her questions about her day at work, and we read the Scriptures together. She gradually opened her heart.

She began to trust me. She realized that I was not going to stop calling her. She opened up and began to share things more personal. We prayed about her concerns, and she began to change. I believe that Joyce began to believe that God the Father loved her and wanted her to have a relationship with Him. Joyce began to see herself differently. Her prayers were prayers of faith, and she gradually began to pray boldly for her ill mother and others members of the family and co-workers. She talked to them about Jesus Christ. Her mother went home to be with the Lord, and Joyce was able to pray for her family at that time.

I shared with her that my father was sick. We would pray for him. After a short illness, he went home to be with the Lord. As we prayed, I noticed she spoke some of the same words that the Holy Spirit had me to say to her during those days she needed comfort. She was very strong during those days. God's peace was resting upon her.

There is a blessing in accepting God's assignment and persisting when challenges accompany the assignment. While the mentor ministers to or blesses the mentee, often the mentee blesses the mentor as well. I received strength from our conversations and prayers. I continued to call Joyce for over a year. One night as we were praying, the Holy Spirit said listen closely and I did. He said she had learned the principles of prayer. "She knows how to pray. It is time for you to pull back and allow her to do it on her own." I felt sad in my spirit. I did not say anything to her about what I had heard that night. I called her the next several nights as usual; however, I finally told her it was time for me to pull back. I told her that I would not call as often; I would call from time to time.

Joyce had a boldness that she never had before. She was praying for healing for people on her job and in her family. She had become an assistant LifeNet Leader and intercessor. The Holy Spirit showed me how to help her but in the meantime, I had grown also. I can tell to this day when things are not what they should be with her, and I pray. I have encouraged her in other areas, and I can tell in my spirit when I need to talk to her. The Father has others speaking into her life. We have a friendship/mentor relationship. God has helped both of us in the process of mentoring.

To be a good mentor, you must be willing to be open and transparent with the mentee. You must be determined to walk with them until you see Christ formed in that area of their life that requires strengthening. According to Bobb Biehl, noted authority on mentoring and leadership, mentoring is a lifelong relationship, in which a mentor helps a protégé reach his or her God-given potential. As a mentor, one asks or must determine "how can I help you" not "what should I teach you?"

One day I received a call at work from my church that there was a person that I needed to meet and mentor. When I got home, I called Cathy Mincey. She did not have much to say except that she expected my call. I asked whether she was a member of Hope and what had happened that day. She was very angry; I could hear it in her voice. I listened to her describe what had happened to her and how angry she became that day. She left the church walking to get away; someone talked her into coming back. I told her that I would call every night, and we would pray. While she said okay, I could tell she was going to require a lot of my time and a lot of prayer. She was quite different from Joyce, so I told Father God that I had to rely on His leading to help me with her.

Cathy was going to Hope Bible College at Hope Christian Church. She had quit her full-time job to go to Bible College. I asked her whether she had saved any money to live on before quitting her job and she said, "No, I believed God would help me." I said okay. At that point, I resisted a response from my thinking. I wanted to understand her thinking on the matter. It was more important to follow or see her decision-making process than to express an opinion on whether God would require or direct anyone to quit a job in such circumstances. My goal was to continue our conversation. I wanted to get to know her and to earn her trust. Sometimes you need to pray before you answer.

I told her I was going to give her $25.00 every time I got paid. She could use the money for anything she wanted. If I did not give it to her, I encouraged her to ask me for the money. She said okay, but I felt like she was not going to ask, and she did not. Pride was a major issue for her, and she felt like she had to fight for other people. If she thought someone was being mistreated, she would speak up for them. She would take on their offenses.

When I called her, she did very little talking, but we did pray. I continued to call and pray, and I would invite her to come and spend time or hang out with me. I never mentioned the word mentoring. I knew she would not like that. Gradually she let her guard down and allowed me to come closer. It was a slow process that required patience and persistence. It was graduation time for the Bible College, and I came to support her. She was surprised that I came. I think that was what did it for her. She still did not know I was mentoring her.

Later, Hope had a women's conference, and they asked me to teach on mentoring. When I taught the class, she was one of the people in attendance. As soon as my session was over, Cathy came to me and said, "I realize now that you have been mentoring me." I laughed and agreed with her conclusion. "Okay, I get it now," she replied. God helper her finish Bible College, and she stayed in her apartment until the end of Bible College. Later, she moved in with a friend.

We continued to talk, pray and hang out together. God has worked many miracles in her life. Today she is a totally different person. She has a compassionate heart. She loves to work with teens, and she is a mighty woman of God. God has used many people to speak words of encouragement into her life. She has grown spiritually. Nothing is impossible for God. If you talk to her today, she is busy working in her church and helping others to grow. She is a mentor. Financially, she has learned how to budget her money.

I continue to serve as a mentor. Each mentee has helped me in some area of my life. It is a blessing to help others. I enjoy being a mentor. I also enjoy and have been blessed by the mentees who have encouraged me. The more you give, the more you receive.

I always encourage the mentee to pray and ask God for directions every day. The Father is the greatest mentor. He guided Jesus who walked side-by-side with the disciples. Jesus chose each disciple; He saw their potential and prayed for them. He taught them how to pray, and He left the Holy Spirit and instructions telling the disciples what to do until He returns.

Do you want to be a mentor?

Are you willing to be a good listener?

Prayer

Father, I thank You today for everyone that is reading this book. Give them a revelation of Your Word. Show them that in helping others we help ourselves. Your Word says, "Give and it shall be given unto you, good measure, pressed down and running over shall men give unto you." That is not just talking about money; it means so much more. The more you give, the more will come back to you in so many ways. Father, we are to encourage one another. I thank You for all the people that have encouraged me over the years. I thank You for saving me and putting the right people in my path.

In Jesus' name, Amen.

Notes and Reflections

How to Maintain an Intimate Relationship with the Father

Maintaining a relationship with anyone requires communication and spending quality time with each other. Communication is very important in maintaining a relationship with anyone—your husband, your friends, co-workers, etc. Merriam-Webster defines communication as "the act or process of using words, sounds, signs, or behaviors to express ideas, thoughts, feelings, etc. to someone else. A message that is given to someone: A letter, telephone call, etc., the technology of the transmission of information (as by print or telecommunication)." All of these represent ways of communicating with others. To maintain a relationship, you must talk to each other on a consistent basis—either in person or by telephone. You remember the last conversation you had with them, the last thing that you shared with each other.

The Father wants us to be the same with Him. He wants you to hear His voice. When you hear His voice, you listen intentionally to hear encouragement, direction, and clarity. You sense His love and peace.

When you do not hear from a friend in a long time, do you wonder how you grew apart? Was there a lack of communication with the other person? Did either of you move to another state? How would the time spent in communication influence the relationship?

Often people who called each other every day, begin to call once a week, monthly, every two to three months, and then once a year. At some point, there's a realization that personal closeness had disappeared. The light bulb comes on, and there is a question about the future. What will happen, can the relationship be restored? You make the first step and call, and when you hear their voice, you remember how close you once were, how much fun you had together and you want that again. All it took was a call on your part. You laugh and talk for hours, and you promise each other that you are going to keep in touch, and you do. You have your friend back. Your relationship is rekindled.

Your relationship with the Father can also be rekindled. He wants to hear your voice; he wants you to talk to Him every day, and He wants to talk to you. He wants you to listen closely to what He has to say. He will always speak, but we are not always listening for what He has to say. We live in a fast-paced world;

everything is going so fast that we don't always want to sit and wait in His presence for an answer. If we don't get an answer to the question that we ask the Father, we automatically do what we think is the right thing to do. We go on autopilot and proceed to carry out our plans not God's plan. We don't spend the time we need in His presence to hear. Our hearing has become dull. And when we do hear, we don't believe that it was Him because we have become so busy that we are not spending time in His Word.

The Holy Spirit is drawing us back to that place of intimacy with the Father. He wants us to know His voice, and when He speaks, we will listen tentatively to what He has to say and respond quickly to what He is saying. Sometimes when we are very active in our churches and our community and keeping up with our children's activities, friends, and our jobs, we can allow those things to cause us not to spend time with the Father. Before we know it, we can't sense His presence like we use to; we don't hear Him speaking like we once did. We feel like something is missing, but we are not exactly sure what it is.

The Father is always waiting for us to return. He is always speaking, but we sometimes are not in a position to hear. Be quick to repent and ask the Father to restore your relationship with Him.

Below are five ways you can maintain your relationship with the Father:

1. Spend quality time reading and studying the Bible

    -   At least 30 minutes a day.

2. Praise and Worship

    -   At least 15 minutes a day

3. Spend time in prayer every day

    -   At least 30 minutes in the morning and 30 minutes at night

4. After you pray or worship, sit and listen quietly with a pad and pen and write down what you hear and date it.

5. Remember the Father is your friend; talk to Him every day and expect Him to talk to you.

Prayer for Forgiveness (If Applicable)

Father, I thank You for the relationship that You and I had. I repent now for not spending the time with You that I did before. Forgive me. Restore the relationship back to what it was before. I'm sorry that I allowed other things to take the place of reading Your Word and talking to You every day. Thank You for forgiving me. I purpose in my heart to come to You every day. In Jesus name, Amen.

Notes and Reflections

Conclusion

Throughout this book, I have shared some of the things the Father has directed me to do. I hope they have encouraged you to have a relationship with Him. We were created to have fellowship with the Father.

When Father God created Adam, it was an intimate moment when He breathed His breath into him. Adam had a close relationship with the Father. They walked and talked to each other every day. That was the ideal relationship. They spent time together (Genesis 2).

Abraham had an intimate relationship with the Father; they made a covenant with one another. God the Father did not destroy Sodom and Gomorrah without talking to Abraham first and sharing what He was going to do (Genesis 17).

David had an intimate relationship with the Father; he danced before the Lord with all of his heart. David is known for having a heart after God. He was not ashamed to praise and worship God.

Moses also had an intimate relationship with the Father. God manifested Himself to Moses in so many different ways so that Moses would know Him. God showed Moses His glory (Exodus 24, 32, 34).

These are just a few of the people in the Bible that had an intimate relationship with the Father. We can have an intimate relationship with the Father also. He wants to walk and talk with us every day; He wants us to acknowledge Him in everything that we do: *Trust in the Lord with all thine heart, and lean not unto thine own understanding. In all thy ways acknowledge Him, and He shall direct thy paths* (Proverbs 3:5-6). God is the same yesterday, today and forever. Allow Him to draw you closer to Him; allow Him to speak to your heart; allow Him to lead you.

To know the Father, you must do the following, not necessarily in the order they are given:

1. Read and study the Word every day.

2. Meditate in the Word every day.

3. Pray

4. Praise and Worship

Conclusion

Praise and Worship is a phrase some use inter-changeably, but the words are actual levels of communicative expressions between the Father and His children. Praise talks about the things He has done for us with a heart of thanksgiving. It can be the open door to worship.

Worship talks about God to God, about who He is. It is more intimate—a greater sense of His presence. There is an exchange of our spirit to His Spirit.

5. Act on the Word - Acting on the Word will cause FAITH to arise in your heart.

6. Expect - Expect The Father to talk to you.

7. Have faith

8. Be consistent and persistent - Set aside a time every day to meet with the Father.

When you spend time praying to the Father, re-member always to wait and listen to what He has to say. Don't spend all the time talking; let Him talk to you. Just sit quietly and listen. As I stated earlier in one of the chapters, listening is a very important skill that we all should develop. Write down what you are hearing and date it. You will be blessed tremendously as you look back over what the Father has said to you and done in your life.

The Father has taught me how to be a mentor, walk in forgiveness, find balance between my family and church life, etc. There is so much joy and peace when you walk with the Father. The Father's love is greater than anything. He loves us so much that He sent His Son, Jesus, to die for our sins.

If you have never received Jesus as your Lord and Savior, you can ask Him now to come into your heart. The only way to the Father is through Jesus, His Son.

Prayer

Pray the following prayer:

Father, in the name of Jesus, according to Romans 10:9-10, "If you confess with your mouth the Lord Jesus and believe in your heart that God has raised Him from the dead, you will be saved. For with the heart one believes unto righteousness, and with the mouth confession is made unto salvation." I ask You to forgive me for my sins and to come into my heart.

Conclusion

I confess You as Lord of my life, and I believe in my heart that Jesus was raised from the dead. Thank You, Jesus, for saving me. Your Word says, "Whosoever shall call on the name of the Lord shall be saved" (Acts 2:21). Thank You, Jesus, for saving me. Help me to live a life that is pleasing to You. I want You to be glorified in my life every day. In Jesus name, Amen.

The Lord bless you and keep you. The Lord make His face shine upon you and be gracious to you; the Lord turn His face toward you and give you peace (Numbers 6:24-26, NIV).

About the Author

Brenda Williams is a woman who exemplifies the love of Christ in every aspect of her life. She is a mentor, an encourager, and more importantly, a woman of faith and prayer. She has a passion to see women healed, delivered, and set free so that they can fulfill the destiny God has ordained for them.

In September 2005, Brenda was ordained an Associate Pastor at Hope Christian Church under the leadership of Bishop Harry R. Jackson, Jr., and serves in several ministries. She has been a teacher in the Delta Force Bible College program and served as head of the Women's Ministry for several years. Brenda, along with several other women, founded Women in Fellowship over 17 years ago and she has been faithfully serving as the President since its conception.

For those who know her well, it is not the titles nor the number of ministries she serves in that makes her the great woman that she is, it is the heart that she has to see people, especially women, whole. Brenda's lifestyle is best summed up in her favorite passage of Scripture, Psalm 34.

Brenda is retired from the Library of Congress Federal Credit Union and has worked in the banking industry for over 35 years. Her devotion and commitment to Christ can be seen as she continues to be a demonstration of the love of God.

Brenda has been happily married for 46 years to Willie Williams and they have two children, one grandchild, and one great grandchild.

Psalm 34

I will bless the Lord at all times; His praise shall continually be in my mouth. ² *My soul shall make its boast in the Lord; The humble shall hear of it and be glad.* ³ *Oh, magnify the Lord with me, And let us exalt His name together.* ⁴ *I sought the Lord, and He heard me, And delivered me from all my fears.* ⁵ *They looked to Him and were radiant, And their faces were not ashamed.* ⁶ *This poor man cried out, and the Lord heard him, And saved him out of all his troubles.* ⁷ *The angel of the Lord encamps all around those who fear Him, And delivers them.* ⁸ *Oh, taste and see that the Lord is good; Blessed is the man who trusts in Him!* ⁹ *Oh, fear the Lord, you His saints! There is no want to those who fear Him.* ¹⁰ *The young lions lack and suffer hunger; But those who seek the Lord shall not lack any good thing.* ¹¹ *Come, you children, listen to me; I will teach you the fear of the Lord. ¹² Who is the man who desires life, And loves many days, that he may see good? ¹³ Keep your tongue from evil, And your lips from speaking deceit. ¹⁴ Depart from evil and do good; Seek peace and pursue it. ¹⁵ The eyes of the Lord are on the righteous, And His ears are open to their cry. ¹⁶ The face of the Lord is against those who do evil, To cut off the remembrance of them from the earth. ¹⁷ The righteous cry out, and the Lord hears, And delivers them out of all their troubles. ¹⁸ The Lord is near to those who have a broken heart, And saves such as have a contrite spirit. ¹⁹ Many are the afflictions of the righteous, But the Lord delivers him out of them all. ²⁰ He guards all his bones; Not one of them is broken. ²¹ Evil shall slay the wicked, And those who hate the righteous shall be condemned. ²² The Lord redeems the soul of His servants, And none of those who trust in Him shall be condemned.*

Contact

To inquire about the author doing book signings, speaking, or ministering at your event, please contact her at

bowilliams1969@gmail.com

For information on ordering copies of *A Walk with the Father*, please contact the author or Kingdom Living Publishing:

Kingdom Living Publishing
P.O. Box 660
Accokeek, Maryland 20607
publish@kingdomlivingbooks.com
(301) 292-9010

CPSIA information can be obtained
at www.ICGtesting.com
Printed in the USA
FFOW05n2227140316